Biblical Answers
To
Everyday Questions

For Women

Stephanie Ahemor

Insight &
Co

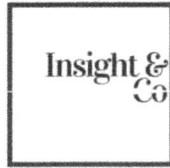

Biblical Answers for Everyday Questions © 2017 by Stephanie Ahemor

Published by Insight and Co Publishing 2017

For information contact the author at:

stephanieahemor@gmail.com

First edition: October 2017

10 9 8 7 6 5 4 3 2 1

ISBN: 978-1-9998767-0-8

DEDICATION

To my wonderful husband. Thank you for your
encouragement, support and love.

To my two patient toddlers. God bless you.

Table of Contents

ACKNOWLEDGMENTS

Thank you God for divine help and providence.

Thank you to all those who encouraged me and supported me with this book.

Ebenezer for standing by me and Kheli for not letting me give up.
Thanks to Casey Elisha for her guidance in the world of writing and publishing.

Thanks to my wonderful proof readers, Ebenezer Ahemor, Lavina Amankwah, Devena Agyei and Kheliwe Njolinjo. Your comments and feedback were greatly appreciated.

And to everyone who confided in me and believed that I had enough wisdom with the help of God to answer their questions, this is for you.

Introduction

I decided to write this book because of all the questions I was asked, after church, in one to one chats and when someone wants to hold a spur of the moment interview session.

I wanted a book that could be referred to again and again which answered questions in all sorts of categories ranging from marriage and family to spiritual life. This book is full of what I believe to be divine wisdom in answer to common, everyday questions. The scriptures are applicable to every area of our lives and they are dynamic, their revelation and application can be different every day.

With this in mind, I hope you are blessed as you read this book.

I would love to hear more of your questions!
So please send them through to me at
stephanieahemor@gmail.com

Parenting and Family

WHAT IS THE BEST WAY TO DISCIPLINE MY CHILDREN?

"Train up a child in the way he should go, and when he is old he will not depart from it"

Proverbs 22:6

The Bible says that **"Foolishness is bound up in the heart of a child; the rod of correction will drive it far from him"** *Proverbs 22:15.*

Foolishness is intrinsic in every child. They are born with it and it has nothing to do with any external factors. Due to this inbuilt foolishness every child needs discipline. Discipline is a crucial factor to succeeding in life and without discipline it is difficult to achieve any level of success.

I write this as someone who pretty much had free reign throughout my childhood and teenage years. Although I thoroughly enjoyed the freedom back then, as an adult I am suffering from the consequences. I still find it difficult to submit to authority nor can I understand why everyone won't agree with me and do as I say!

As an adult I have spent much time being corrected and rebuked. The discipline has had to be instilled in me at one stage or another in life. Believe me, it is much harder to learn discipline and take correction as a stubborn and independent adult than it is as a more compliant, easy-going child.

Every child is different, so what works in terms of discipline for one child may not work for another. My two daughters, although close in age, are disciplined in different ways because they respond differently. Every child has a different personality. Be aware of this. Be careful not to crush their spirit because someone has said that your child should behave in a certain way.

My eldest daughter is full of energy and has a larger than life personality. As parents, my husband and I, have to be quite strict with her to keep her boundless energy within safe parameters. However, we are also acutely aware that God has packaged all aspects of her for the great destiny she is to fulfill. Therefore we are careful not to suppress her personality but put boundaries in place to allow her to grow up to be the best person she can be.

Correct your child in love. Although it may feel harsh at the time of the discipline, the outcome will be far greater and the reward worth it. Remember, **" the one who loves their children is careful to discipline them."** (*Proverbs 13:24 NIV*).

Discipline helps one to learn accountability and to realise that there are consequences to actions, a reaction to every action. Discipline brings wisdom (*Proverbs 29:15*) and wisdom brings protection (*Proverbs 4:6*). To accomplish anything in life, discipline is required to set the goal and stay on course to achieve it.

"Listen to advice and accept discipline, and at the end you will be counted among the wise."
Proverbs 19:20

Whenever I feel frustrated by circumstances or by my children's behaviour, I remember that **" I can do all things**

through Christ who strengthens me" (*Philippians 4:6*) to raise them in a Godly manner.

> Discipline your children according to their differing needs, not according to how other people think your children should behave.

Stephanie Ahemor

The Four Temperaments

(Based on 'I love you, but why are we so different?' Tim LaHaye, 1991)

The temperaments comes from the study of human behavior that suggests that we all have inherited behavioral tendencies which can be split into the four personality types detailed below.

Suzy Sanguine

Ms Sanguine is a warm and outgoing personality. A natural extrovert, she is the life and soul of any gathering or party. She never lacks friends and her exuberant retelling of stories has listeners hanging on to her every word.

The greatest weakness of Suzy Sanguine is her lack of discipline which can lead to her being unreliable and dishonest. Although she can be compassionate towards others, she can also be manipulative. If Suzy can overcome her weaknesses and learn to be consistent then there is no limit to her reaching her potential.

Chloe Choleric

Chloe is a goal-orientated, active and strong-willed type who is able to lead others. Life is full of action and activity fueled by her endless plans and ambitions. She is full of determination and goes on to succeed where others fail, not because she is cleverer but because her persistence takes her through.

However, Chloe Choleric is not able to easily sympathise with others, nor is she moved by displays of emotion. Her most serious weakness is anger which can be used as a weapon to manipulate others. With the help of the Holy Spirit she can be guided towards gentleness and use her talent and skills to pioneer great ventures.

Melanie Melancholy

She has a rich temperament. She is gifted, analytical and a self-sacrificing type. Melanie enjoys art and music, she a faithful friend and her perfectionism prevents her from letting people down. Her analytical ability allows her to forecast any dangers ahead when planning projects.

The biggest weaknesses of the melancholic are criticism and negativity. Due to this, it is difficult for her to start a project as she can only see potential failure; she can also quench the ideas of others. Due to her sacrificial nature, Melanie is able to pursue a career which requires long and intense periods of study. She is also able to produce great works although it may be followed by periods of depression.

If with the help of the Holy Spirit, the melancholic is able to fight her pessimistic nature, she will be able to accomplish much in her life.

Felicia Phlegmatic

Felicia is the most likeable of the temperaments. She is calm, easy-going and friendly, it is difficult to ruffle her feathers. Although she displays a cool, calm and almost shy personality, beneath she has a range of capabilities. The phlegmatic is able to find humour in all situations and is a natural peacemaker.

Her biggest weakness is a lack of motivation. She will not volunteer herself for leadership roles of her own volition but when put forward for them makes an excellent leader. She can be sluggish and seem to lack drive and ambition. Her innate stubbornness is covered by politeness; she will cover her refusal to fulfill a demand by simply side-stepping it or by employing delay tactics.

Overall, she is a gentle person who prefers to hang back and work at her own pace.

I AM ABOUT TO MARRY BUT HAVE CHILDREN FROM A PREVIOUS RELATIONSHIP. HOW DO I CREATE A COHESIVE BLENDED FAMILY?

"Joseph also went up...to be registered with Mary, his betrothed wife, who was with child"

Luke 2:4,5

Firstly, congratulations on your upcoming nuptials. After past failed relationships, it is easy to think that you'll never fall in love again or that no one will accept you as you are now, following the experiences and trials you have been through. Take your time when introducing your families. You have the rest of your lives to spend together so there's no need to rush.

Make prayer a priority (*Philippians 4:6*). The only way to navigate this road and to make the best decisions in wisdom, is to hear from God. Pray about your marriage daily; pray for your future spouse, their career, their family, their ministry, their housing, pray about anything that concerns them.

Recognise that the path will not be entirely smooth. You are two different people coming from different backgrounds and different family upbringings. Therefore you may not see eye to eye on certain routines such as whether to wash dishes straight after preparing a meal or whether it is ok to leave them until the next morning. A level of compromise and flexibility is needed in order to blend two families together.

Take your time to introduce your children to your partner. Once a relationship has been established between your children and partner it can be difficult and complex to undo, particularly if the relationship between yourself and your partner, for whatever reason fails to proceed.

Maintain an open forum between yourself, your children, your partner and their children. Perhaps have weekly informal dinners or game nights where everyone can meet in a low pressure environment. Allow everyone to communicate their feelings and thoughts on anything that is happening. Give them a safe space to express themselves to you. This allows you to address any issues that may arise and prevent resentment from brewing.

Reassure your children that their non-resident parent is not being replaced by your partner. Reassure them that they are loved and nothing and no-one will ever replace the relationship they have with the parent they don't live with.

Set boundaries. Be careful not to blur lines. Keep what is intended for marriage, for marriage. Perhaps, because you may be more mature or have life experience you feel that it is okay to sleep together before marriage. It isn't. The same principles from the Bible still apply. Don't have sex before marriage, don't move in together prematurely, wait until the wedding day to bring two families together as one, God will surely favour you.

Although you may have been hurt by past relationships, don't bring the patterns of past relationships into this new relationship.

"Nor do they put new wine into old wineskins, or else the wineskins break, the wine is spilled, and the wineskins are ruined... "

Matthew 9:17

Practice forgiveness. Unforgiveness is like drinking poison and expecting the other person to die. Holding on to the pain and bitterness causes you hurt and does not allow you to move on, whilst the person who wronged you has no idea of the impact and pain they are continuing to cause you. It is not your fiancé's fault that your ex-boyfriend wronged you in the past.

"You are a new creation in Christ, old things have passed away, and all things have become new." (*2 Corinthians 5:17*)

Celebrate! Enjoy your new relationship and go on to have a happy and successful marriage with the help of God. You are blessed!

> Create an open forum where everyone is free to speak, perhaps a relaxed family dinner where all of the family are able to meet.

HOW CAN I BE A BETTER DAUGHTER?

"Let your father and your mother be glad and let her who bore you rejoice"

Proverbs 23:25

There are instances where people come from toxic backgrounds and toxic families, that is the reality of it. For those who have come from such backgrounds, when they have managed to escape from the tangled mess that is their youth, the general idea is to never go back and this can mean cutting off communication in order to stop any reminders of a painful past.

Distance is definitely needed to escape from and avoid negative habits and harmful thought patterns but we must still remember that the Bible says 'Honour your mother and father. This is the first commandment with promise' (*Ephesians 6:2,3*). If we honour our parents then we have long life. Honouring our parents does not necessarily have to mean liking them but we must continue to love them. When a father has been absent for most of one's life, how can a person compel themselves to like this virtual stranger?

Let us honour our parents by being respectful of them, by maintaining a cordial relationship wherever possible and by letting bitterness and hurt towards them dissolve. This does as much good to us as it does to them.

Open up the lines of communication and allow any past hurts to fade away. Put the onus on yourself to contact them, call and visit when you can. Your relationship with your parent when you are both adults is very different to how it was when you were a child. You are no longer a scared, vulnerable child. You are now in a position to build up a relationship with your parent based on mutual respect and with maturity you may be better able to understand their decision making process for the actions they took when you were a child.

Practice forgiveness. Allow your heart to be healed of rejection and brokenness. Love your parents like the Father loves us. Although your upbringing may not have been ideal, remember it is those circumstances that led you to being the unique and creative human being you are today.

Rejoice in all things knowing that you have a heavenly Father who is always there for you and cannot let you down.

> Practice forgiveness towards your parents
> for any hurt they may have caused you.

Classic West African Tomato Stew

Ingredients

1 white onion	1 scotch bonnet pepper
3 tins of plum tomatoes	1 bay leaf
1 tbsp tomato puree	½ tsp of salt
2 Maggi cubes	Sunflower or vegetable oil
1 cm cube of ginger	Cooked meat/fish
2 garlic cloves	

Method

1. Gently heat enough oil to cover the bottom of a large pot whilst finely dicing onion.
2. Blend tinned tomatoes, roughly peeled and chopped garlic and ginger, and scotch bonnet to taste until the mixture is smooth and few tomato seeds are visible.
3. Add the onion to the oil on low heat and fry gently for a few minutes until onions are caramelized.
4. Add a large tablespoon of tomato puree and fry for 2-3 minutes until the onion begins to brown at the edges of the pan.
5. Pour the blended tomato mixture into the pan.
6. Allow the mixture to simmer for 15-20 minutes
7. Add salt, the bay leaf and Maggi cubes to season
8. Continuing simmering the mixture for a further 10 minutes.

9. Add cooked meat or fish of your choice such as chicken drumsticks or diced goat/lamb/beef. A tin of corned beef can be crumbled in as an alternative, eggs can be added or stirred in or the stew can be left plain.
10. Let the mixture continue to simmer to absorb the flavours of whatever you've added.
11. When the oil rises to the top of the stew and the stew has thickened, it is done. Enjoy!

Marriage

WHAT SHOULD I KNOW ABOUT MY POTENTIAL SPOUSE BEFORE I SAY 'I DO'?

"…they ask me things that I do not know"

Psalm 35:11

I often wonder why it is that couples are married and are experiencing frustration after years of marriage because the man doesn't want to have children and the woman does. She hopes to persuade him to have 'just one', he hopes that she will forget the whole fantasy. They are both stuck in a stalemate, in a hostile environment in their own homes.

There are questions that need to be asked before you say 'I do'. Once you make that commitment you cannot backtrack. If you are forearmed with knowledge, then together you and your future spouse can work through any issues that arise with Godly counsel and prayer.

Some questions to ask are:

- Is that your real name?
- What is your age?
- Do you have any children?
- Have you changed gender before?
- What is your relationship like with your mother and father?
- What is your relationship like with your brothers and sisters?
- Do you want to have children? If so, how many?
- Have you been unfaithful in a relationship before?
- Have you left a husband/wife behind somewhere?
- What is the state of your finances?
- Are you healthy/are there any health conditions you need to disclose to me?
- What does being a Christian mean to you?
- What was your upbringing like?
- Have you ever been abused?
- What are your goals in life?

They say that forewarned is forearmed. The more you know about your future spouse the better equipped you'll be in marriage to work together as one cohesive unit.

Don't be scared to ask questions! The experiences your intended spouse has been through has shaped who they are today. Share those experiences with each other.

Wedding Planning Timeline

Congratulations! You're engaged!

12 MONTHS TO GO

- Book venue for reception
- Book church or registry office
- Start looking at dresses

10 MONTHS TO GO

- Book wedding planner if needed
- Book photographer/videographer
- Book DJ
- Write guest list

9 MONTHS TO GO

- Order dress
- Taste cakes and book
- Book florist
- Book decorator if needed
- Register for gifts
- Get hair and make-up trials

6 MONTHS TO GO

- Confirm catering

- Get invitations designed
- Shop for bridesmaid dresses
- Arrange wedding cars
- Book marriage counselling

4 MONTHS TO GO

- Send out invitations
- Buy groom's and groomsmen attire
- Book entertainment
- Book hair and make up artists
- Organise dress fittings
- Buy rings

8 WEEKS TO GO

- Attend dress fitting
- Choose music
- Finalise readings and order of service
- Follow up with those who haven't RSVP'd
- Reconfirm bookings with all vendors

3 WEEKS TO GO

- Arrange seating plan
- Book dress rehearsal

1 WEEK TO GO

- Set apart time to fast and pray with your groom

- Arrange manicure

- Attend dress rehearsal

- Get engagement ring cleaned

- Delegate any last minute tasks

1 DAY TO GO

- Have an early night and rest well ahead of tomorrow. Don't panic, it will all be fine on the day.

HOW DO I PREPARE TO BE A WIFE?

"He who finds a wife finds a good thing,
And obtains favor from the Lord."

Proverbs 18:22

Someone recently approached me and said: "I want you to teach me how to be a wife." What?! I was bewildered, I was flabbergasted. How would I undertake such a thing, where would I start? After some thinking I decided to consult the well-known chapter in the Bible which many of us have looked on when needing to draw inspiration from a formidable and talented God-fearing woman. Nothing encompasses the attributes of the ideal woman better than the Word of God, so here it is, the person specification of a Proverbs 31 woman.

The Proverbs 31 woman or wife:

- Has a noble character
- Is worth more than precious jewels
- Is trustworthy
- Does good things for her husband

- Enjoys her work
- Finds the best bargains
- Cooks for her family
- Is business minded
- Reinvests her profits
- Works all hours
- Is creative
- Is charitable and generous
- Plans ahead
- Can sew and mend
- Is well dressed
- Respects her husband
- Has a trade
- Is strong
- Is dignified
- Is cheerful and full of laughter
- Is not worried by adversity
- Speaks wisdom
- Has the word of God in her mouth
- Manages and cares for her household
- Is not lazy
- She is blessed

- Is deserving of praise
- Is God-fearing
- Is honourable

The Proverbs 31 woman is the best scriptural example of a multi-talented, multi-faceted woman who was able to look after her family whilst taking care of all her other interests. She is a good character study for a model wife. The scriptures are the breath of God (*2 Timothy 3:16*) therefore they are alive and new revelations can be found in them all the time. Something you read in the scriptures may not give you a great insight today but will unveil a unique revelation tomorrow, that is why it is important to keep hearing the word. Study this woman again and again and a new aspect of her life can reach out to you and compel you to add that skill to your own life.

A line that recently jumped out to me from the description of the Proverbs 31 woman is that she **'does not eat the bread of idleness'**. This has motivated me to not be lazy and I've realised that's it not a new thing to stay up late at night finishing off work! She has done it already and I can do it too.

> Don't worry about being perfect, it's not
> possible. Concentrate instead on bringing out
> the best in yourself.

Four types of Love

The word 'love' translated into English in the Bible stems from four Greek words which all mean love: *Eros; Storge, Phileo* and *Agape*.

Eros love is a romantic love. The love that attracts you to your partner, it is a physical attraction and often culminates in a physical exercise, sex because of the feelings induced when you admire the beauty of your partner.

Phileo is defined as brotherly love.

Storge is the type of love that a parent has for a child.

Agape is unconditional love. It is the type of love that God has for us. The Bible says we love God because He first loved us (1 John 4:19).

WHY SHOULDN'T I HAVE SEX BEFORE MARRIAGE?

"Do not stir up nor awaken love

Until it pleases."

Songs of Solomon 2:7

In these modern times it may seem like that there is no longer any reason to continue following ancient laws such as not having sex before marriage. However, God is still the same yesterday, today and forever so the precepts that are in the Bible are still the same ones we are expected to live by today. They are just as relevant to us now as they were thousands of years ago.

Here are some reasons why you should wait until marriage to have sex and be physically intimate with your partner.

1. It prematurely creates one flesh

"Therefore a man shall leave his father and mother and be joined to his wife, and they shall become one flesh."

Genesis 2:24

Sex brings about the connection of two people; body, soul and spirit into one flesh. This undertaking is not to be underestimated. By having sex with someone you are joining your souls together and to separate the two again is difficult and cannot be achieved superficially i.e by ending the relationship and no longer having sex. A tie still remains between the two of you and sometimes deliverance is required to break that tie.

2. It creates false intimacy

"Do not stir up nor awaken love

Until it pleases."

Songs of Solomon 8:4

Having sex before marriage creates false intimacy in that you believe that the two of you are closer than you really are. Because you are joining yourselves together in a physical experience you falsely think that you know everything about this person and that the physical act of sex is a mirror for the emotional counterpart of love. It can be heartbreaking to later find out that whilst you were in love, your sexual partner was only experiencing lust. When a couple do not have sex during courtship, that time and energy is used to explore each and find out what makes each other tick. Intimacy is built in the meeting of minds and a deep friendship is able to be built, which provides a solid foundation for marriage to rest upon.

3. It creates trust issues

"Marriage is honorable among all, and the bed undefiled; but fornicators and adulterers God will judge."

Hebrews 13:4

Couples who have sex before marriage and later go onto to marry often go on to have trust issues during their marriage. This is because if the couple were not able to keep their hands off each other and abstain during the courtship period then doubts arise later on during the marriage as each spouse thinks if their partner just couldn't wait and just couldn't help themselves before marriage, what's to say they're not currently cheating whilst claiming to be working late in the office?

The fact that a couple are able to abstain before marriage makes it less likely that will commit adultery later as they have proven that they have been able to resist temptation in times past. This does not mean they are a saint however! With enough persistence anyone can fall.

It's a good testimony to be able to wait until marriage. You don't know who you will counsel in later years and you will able to tell them that it is not impossible you were able to wait and so they can too. Don't be unrealistic, you are a human being with human feelings and emotions. Don't set a wedding date two years away if you know you will find it difficult to keep from being tempted and consummating the relationship before marriage. As you prepare for the wedding, set time apart with your fiancé to regularly pray into the marriage and into your future, it will pay off.

> Create a regular time to pray and fast with your fiancé in preparation towards your wedding. Spiritual preparation is essential for a successful marriage.

MY HUSBAND HAS CHEATED ON ME. HOW DO I MOVE PAST THIS?

"...The Lord is near to those with a broken heart..."

Psalm 34:18

It starts with making a conscious decision that you are going to fight for your marriage. I hope that does not sound condescending. Adultery is extremely painful and shatters both marriage and family life, and seeps negatively into every area of your life. What you believed to be true is no longer true and it is outstanding and shocking to think that the person you loved and trusted has been capable of conducting the ultimate betrayal behind your back.

You need to fight for your marriage. Let him know that you are not about to give up. Talk to each other, open up the lines of communication. Express what you feel and what you have been going through. It may be ugly but it will also be cathartic.

Spend time in prayer. Seek spiritual counseling, speak to

your Christian brother or sister, your Pastor or Minister. People commit adultery and are able to restore their marriage. It may have been a one off incident that will not happen again. Divorce should be seen as the last resort if your spouse is not willing or able to change.

Adultery is a painful experience but know that the relationship can be restored and trust can be rebuilt. Bring life back into the relationship. Make time for each other as you start anew.

If God can raise people from the dead then He can put life back into your marriage, He can put life back into your relationship.

The Bible says:

"Therefore confess your sins to each other and pray for each other so that you may be healed. The prayer of a righteous person is powerful and effective."

James 5:16

As your husband speaks to you and confesses everything

that has been going on, pray for him and pray for yourself. Your prayers will help you to heal from feelings of inadequacy, bitterness and loneliness.

Your marriage can work! Look forward to the coming years which will be filled with joy and laughter. God is restoring peace back into your home.

Seek counseling from reputable counsellors.

Additional resources

<u>Books</u>

200 questions you must ask, investigate and know before

you say I do

Michael and Bernice Hutton-Wood

Household

HOW DO I BUILD A HOME FOR MY FAMILY?

"Through wisdom a house is built and by understanding it is established. By knowledge the rooms are filled with all precious and pleasant riches"

Proverbs 24:3,4

The Bible says that a wise woman builds her house but the foolish woman tears it down with her hands. The atmosphere in a home is largely down to the woman, whether it be a peaceful home or a home full of contention and strife. It is clear when you step into a home which is prayed in often, as the atmosphere is light and comforting. When you enter a home where the inhabitants are constantly upset and fighting, then you can sense the tension and are often anxious to leave the home as soon as possible.

Here are some things you can do to create a Godly atmosphere at home:

Be thankful

Oh, give thanks to the Lord, for He is good! For His mercy endures forever.

Psalm 136:1

Don't complain/murmur

"And all the children of Israel complained against Moses and Aaron, and the whole congregation said to them, "If only we had died in the land of Egypt! Or if only we had died in this wilderness!"

Numbers 14:2

Be joyful

"Rejoice always"

1 Thessalonians 5:16

Praise God

"Praise the Lord!

Praise God in His sanctuary;

Praise Him in His mighty firmament!

Let everything that has breath praise the Lord.

Praise the Lord!"

Psalm 150:1,6

Don't be contentious

"It is better to dwell in a corner of a housetop,

Than in a house shared with a contentious woman."

Proverbs 25:24

Be encouraging

"Therefore encourage one another and build each other

up, just as in fact you are doing."

1 Thessalonians 5:11 (NIV)

Pray always

"Pray without ceasing"

1 Thessalonians 5:17

Speak life

"Death and life are in the power of the tongue"

Proverbs 18:21

Sing songs

"Praise the Lord!

Sing to the Lord a new song,

And His praise in the assembly of saints.

Let the saints be joyful in glory;

Let them sing aloud on their beds."

Psalm 150:1,5

Let the sweet perfume of peace and joy permeate through your home. Let it always be a pleasure and a happy experience for everyone who enters through your door.

> Start your day with praising God, even as you get ready in the morning. What a delightful way to start the day.

I WANT TO RELOCATE. HOW DO I KNOW WHERE TO LIVE?

"Now the Lord had said to Abram: Get out of your country, from your family and from your father's house, to a land that I will show you"

Genesis 12:1

As I write this my family and I are preparing to relocate. We are sorting out the logistics of moving to a new town and everything it entails, finding accommodation, new jobs and nurseries.

At this point nothing is set in stone and I don't know whether we will actually make the move or not but I do know that I am ok with whatever the outcome is going to be. It took a long time and quite a dramatic event for me to get to this point, but now I can be like Ruth and say, **"Where you go, I will go and where you stay I will stay"** *Ruth 1:16.* The decision to relocate wasn't down to me. It was my husband who decided he wanted to live elsewhere and I protested for two years before I finally agreed. I realised that what I thought was important to me wasn't actually that important. I cited my support network as one of the reasons I couldn't leave London but have since realised that I see my family infrequently although we all live in the same city. It is often my friends and church family that I rely on for help.

I also didn't want to leave because I was stable here. Well I can tell you that all of that stability was thrown out of the window when we moved into a new build apartment which promptly burnt down three weeks after moving in. After living in hotels and temporary accommodation with our two very young children (the youngest celebrated her 1st birthday in the hotel room we were living in) I came to the conclusion that children are adaptable and cheerful each day as long as you show them plenty of love. If, as a family, we were able to survive and even thrive from living in one room for 2 months with no cooking facilities then moving from one UK city to another was hardly going to harm us.

Fears quenched, I turned to my husband and said 'Yes I'm ready to go wherever you want to go. We will all follow you'.

Although it wasn't my decision to relocate, I know that I am instrumental in making it happen. My husband's decision is based on knowing that this is what God has called him to do in the next phase of his life. I am willing to yield to that plan as I'm not willing for another disaster to happen to change my thinking!

> Be open minded to the path that God wants
> you to take.

SHOULD I RENT OR BUY A HOUSE?

"For which of you, intending to build a tower does not sit down first and count the cost, whether he has enough to finish it"

Luke 14:28

Whilst not everyone has the financial opportunity to buy a home there are many advantages to buying a home over renting.

- Security-private renting can be uncertain.
- Monthly payments are often cheaper with a mortgage compared to rent
- Equity- buying a house is an investment
- Can decorate a bought home in any way you wish

Even if you are not in a position to buy a house now, make it a long-term goal and work towards it by keeping things in order.

- Pay credit cards and bills on time to keep your credit score healthy.
- Download your credit score for free from Experian to find out about any open credit facilities you may not know about. I once found out that I had £500 of available credit on a credit card I knew nothing about. It had been opened when I began university and the card was never sent to me. Too much available credit can harm your credit score.
- Cut back on spending. For example decrease the amount you spend on takeaways and cook from scratch more often. Look for vouchers online when making purchases. Consider buying clothes from charity shops.
- Pay off any debt.
- Research government initiatives that are aimed at helping people to buy a house. Consider opening a help to buy ISA or research buying a property through shared ownership.
- Start saving for a deposit!

Download a credit report for free from Experian.

HOW I BUDGET AND MANAGE FINANCES FOR MY HOUSEHOLD?

"The plans of the diligent lead surely to plenty but those of everyone who is hasty surely to poverty"

Proverbs 21:5

It is a lot of responsibility to manage the finances and budget for the entire household. Here are some tips to help you excel in that responsibility.

- Meal plan. Meal planning not only helps you to keep the food for your family organised but allows you to save money as you are grocery shopping with a plan in mind. This should help you to avoid impulse purchases such as a new flavour chocolate bar or a two for one offer which is actually not the bargain it seems.

- Consider shopping at discount supermarkets such as Aldi and Lidl. You can make significant savings on the cost of grocery shopping in those shops as their streamlined approach to product lines and promotions means that they are able to pass on the savings to their customers.

- Try clothes shopping in charity shops or buying clothes online from online auctioneer Ebay. Through Ebay you can buy clothes from China but beware of lengthy shipping times and note that the quality of the clothes may not stand up to the pictures shown.

- Create a system to keep on top of paperwork. Keep an expanding file and label each section i.e. bills, insurance, school letters etc.

- Note when direct debits are coming out of your account and when other bills need to be paid.

- Look at your bank statements to keep an eye on spending

- Download or create a budget spreadsheet so that you can easily allocate your income to different activities.

Get your family on board to help. You don't have to manage everything alone.

Sell unwanted items on eBay or at car boot sales.

Upcycle unloved pieces of furniture to give them a

new lease of life.

I AM THOUSANDS OF POUNDS IN DEBT. HOW DO I GET OUT OF THIS?

"The rich rules over the poor,
And the borrower is servant to the lender."

Proverbs 22:7

First of all don't panic. It's good that you've been able to admit that there is a problem, now you can find help.

Contact a debt charity such as StepChange or Christians Against Poverty (CAP). They will not judge you but will help you to go through your income and outgoings and assist you in managing your creditors perhaps by creating a reduced payment plan.

Next, prioritise your payments. Pay the essentials first such as rent/mortgage. Then food, council tax, utility bills such as gas and electricity, insurance, childcare and phones. Followed by car payments, credit cards and unsecured debts. Find out if you're eligible for any benefits.

Ask God to help you control your spending. Honour God with your tithes even in the midst of these difficult circumstances. And ultimately be a sower. You are tapping into and activating Kingdom principles when you sow.

In Genesis 26 we learn that there was a great famine in the land. In the same land that was experiencing famine Isaac sowed.

The Bible says:

"Then Isaac sowed in that land, and reaped in the same year a hundredfold; and the Lord blessed him. The man began to prosper, and continued prospering until he became very prosperous"

Genesis 26:12,13

In spite of what he saw around him Isaac sowed and was able to become so wealthy that he became the subject of envy of the Philistines.

Remember, **"Do not be deceived, God is not mocked, for**

whatever a man sows, that he will also reap" (*Galatians 6:7*).

That means you cannot reap what you do not sow! Keep sowing, God will bring you out of these difficult times.

> Stop borrowing and prioritise paying off accumulated debt.

Stephanie Ahemor

Meal Planner

Day	Breakfast	Lunch	Snacks	Dinner
Monday				
Tuesday				
Wednesday				
Thursday				
Friday				
Saturday				
Sunday				

Shopping List:

HOW DO I CREATE A HOSPITABLE ENVIRONMENT FOR GUESTS?

"Do not forget to show hospitality to strangers, for by so doing some people have shown hospitality to angels without knowing it."

Hebrews 13:2 (NIV)

I have to admit that I'm not the most hospitable of hosts. I try my best but often have to be prompted to get my guests drinks or notice when I need to add an extra portion of food to their plates.

I believe it is a good skill to be hospitable and it is important to have a welcoming, homely environment to welcome people into. Whenever I go into the home of a friend and come away feeling well nourished, whether through words or food then I always take mental notes to ensure that I can add to the positive experience of any guests in my home.

I have a friend who always has a well-stocked supply of

food in her home. This means she is able to cater for unexpected guests ranging from 1 person to 30 people all without breaking a sweat.

Some of the types of food she keeps in her home are boxes of spring rolls, frozen chicken wings and potato wedges, as well as a well-stocked supply of bottled and/or canned drinks. This is relatively inexpensive and items can be kept in the freezer or the cupboard.

I have another friend who always makes me feel so comfortable in her home and never an imposition. She always accommodates myself and my children without fuss. This is such an important factor in being a good host.

Whenever I think of hospitality in the Bible I think of Elijah and the widow of Zarephath. (*1 Kings 7:8-16*). At this time in his life, Elijah received his provisions, i.e. food and water, from God as there was a drought in the land.

When God sent Elijah, He told Elijah **"I have commanded a widow to provide for you"**. When Elijah asked the widow to get him a cup of water she willingly obliged but when he asked her for a morsel of bread she turned back and protested. As the prophet issued a prophetic word, she obeyed and later received a testimony.

"So she went away and did according to the word of Elijah; and she and he and her household ate for many days. The bin of flour was not used up, nor did the jar of oil run dry, according to the word of the Lord which He spoke by Elijah."
1 Kings 17:15,16

Jesus said that in those days there were many widows in Zarephath but Elijah was sent to only one (*Luke 4:25,26*). Due to the widow's obedience in providing for the man of God, she flourished where other widows perished. The blessing that stemmed from her giving bread to Elijah and showing kindness to him extended to the point of Elijah reviving her son when he was sick onto death.

Hospitality is defined as the "friendly and generous reception and entertainment of guests, visitors, or strangers".

Express the love of God to everyone you meet and good hospitality will flow through you.

> Treat your guests the way you
> would like to be treated; make
> them feel at home.

HOW DO I KEEP MY HOME CLEAN?

"Therefore lay aside all filthiness..."

James 1:21

I'll confess I'm no domestic goddess. I try my best but I'm not always on top of household chores, with two young children my house can frequently be untidy.

My best tip is acquire plenty of storage. If everything has a place then it can be tided there. Children can also help with putting away their toys if they know where everything belongs. Now that everything is off the floor and the surfaces are uncluttered you can begin cleaning.

There are several leading ladies in the cleaning world who publish routines and have techniques to keep the home clean.

Flylady recommends allocating a day to cleaning each room of the house i.e. bathrooms on Monday, bedrooms on Tuesday as well as other small daily tasks such as always having a clean sink. Marie Kondo of, The Life Changing Magic of Tidying fame, advocates decluttering. By having less material things in your home it will be easier to keep your home tidy and neat.

Find whichever way works best for you. Just do it frequently enough to ensure you keep on top of all household tasks. It doesn't take long before the laundry spirals out of control (such as my own mountain of clean clothes, which have yet to, and may never be put away).

If everyone plays their part in keeping the house tidy then it should reduce some of the pressure on you. Everyone can pitch in to help, even children can put dirty clothes in the laundry basket and plates in the kitchen.

Life is too short, so get a cleaner, get a dishwasher or just close the kitchen door. There's no use in spending all of your time stressing over a bit of mess.

Share chores amongst
members of the house, don't
let resentment build.

Stephanie Ahemor

Cleaning Schedule

Everyday

oWash dishes/empty dishwasher

oWipe kitchen sink, counter and surfaces

oMake beds

oSweep floors

oQuick tidy up of cluttered surfaces and floors

oLaundry

oWipe bathroom sink and surfaces

oEmpty bins

Monday [Living room]

- o Tidy up any clutter
- o Organise toys
- o Straighten cushions
- o Dust surfaces

Tuesday [Bedrooms]

- o Change bedding
- o Clean floors
- o Wipe down any surfaces
- o Pick up stray clothes and put in laundry basket
- o Fold and put away clean clothes

Wednesday [Kitchen]

- Clean hob
- Wipe inside of microwave and outside of kettle
- Throw expired food in fridge away and wipe inside of fridge
- Clean sink and counters
- Wipe outside of cupboards and cabinets
- Sweep and mop floor

Thursday [Bathrooms]

- Clean sinks and countertops
- Clean bath/shower
- Clean toilet
- Empty bins
- Wash bath mats
- Sweep and mop floor

Friday [Hallway, Office, Stairs, Misc]

- Tidy up coats and shoes
- Tidy desk
- Replace books onto shelves
- Water plants

Saturday [Outside]

- Organise garage
- Tend to plants
- Sweep yard
- Mow grass if necessary

HOW CAN I BE A GOOD OR BETTER FRIEND?

"As iron sharpens iron, so a man sharpens the countenance of his friend."

Proverbs 27:17

A good friend helps you to become a better person. They should build you up and encourage you. Their unique perspective should inspire you to new and exciting ideas. You should pull each other up, not tear each other down. But firstly you must be aware of who is a friend. Not everyone who you consider to be a friend is actually a friend.

When I first started writing the answer to this question, I realised that what I actually wanted to discuss was the importance of being careful of the company that you keep.

Proverbs 13:20 says: **"He who walks with wise men will be wise, but the companion of fools will be destroyed."**

I once heard a man of God say, 'The company you keep matters'. The friends you have can lead to your rising or downfall.

God told Abraham to leave his father's house and his family to go to a land where he would be made into a great nation. Although Abraham followed God's instruction, he didn't fully obey as he took his nephew Lot on the journey with him.

"Abram was very rich in livestock, in silver and in gold"
Genesis 13:2

Unfortunately, there was strife between the herdsmen of Abraham and Lot because their combined possessions were too great to be contained in one land. The manifestation of the blessing God had previously issued began to be enacted after Abraham had separated from the wrong company.

"**And the Lord said to Abram, after Lot had separated from him: "Lift your eyes now and look from the place where you are—northward, southward, eastward, and westward; for all the land which you see I give to you and your descendants forever. And I will make your** descendants as the dust of the earth; so that if a man could number the dust of the earth, then your descendants also could be numbered. Arise, walk in the land through its length and its width, for I give it to you."

Genesis 13:14-17

Not everyone wants the best for you and their negativity can prevent you from going to great places in life. A good friend should encourage and inspire you to become the best person you can.

"As iron sharpens iron, so a man sharpens the countenance of his friend."

Proverbs 27:17

So exercise wisdom when considering your friends, **"For as he thinks in his heart, so is he"** *Proverbs 23:7*. Consider what is really in your friend's heart concerning you.

> Choose your friends wisely and in prayer.

ADDITIONAL RESOURCES

Websites

Debt Charities

StepChange

www.stepchange.org

Christians Against Poverty

https://capuk.org

Budgeting Advice

MoneySavingExpert

www.moneysavingexpert.com

MoneyMagpie

www.moneymagpie.com

Credit Score

Experian

www.experian.com

Stephanie Ahemor

<u>Books</u>

The Life-Changing Magic of Tidying

Marie Kondo

Work Life

HOW DO I DEVELOP MY CAREER?

"…no I worked harder than all of them, yet not I but the grace of God that was within me"

2 Corinthians 15:10

Identify avenues of promotion in your current workplace. Read through the intranet or current policy, look at the work hierarchy to see the stepping stones of where you can advance to next.

Get a workplace mentor, most employers offer this scheme as a way of introducing an alternative form of learning and guidance for the mentee.

Undertake study or work towards qualifications that will advance or further your career. In some careers the only way to climb the career ladder is to pass exams such as CIPD in HR or ACCA in accounting. In other careers the best way to advance is through gaining more knowledge through work experience.

Keep up with current trends, read around your industry. Volunteer on new projects or areas of work whilst in your current role so that you can gain experience to add to your CV.

Apply for new jobs if there are no opportunities for promotion in your current workplace.

If you are considering a career change then try getting experience in your potential field. Take annual leave from work and get a week or two of work experience in your chosen field. Contact those who are already in the field and ask for advice. If you don't ask, you don't get. Find out what re-training, if any, is needed.

In the Bible, Daniel underwent a period of training before he went through examinations and an interview. Daniel and the other Hebrew men passed successfully and were all appointed to serve before the King (*Daniel 1*). Daniel stood out because he trusted in God. When he rejected the portion of the King's delicacies he knew that God was able to keep him. God gave Daniel favour before the Chief of Staff so that his requests were accommodated. Daniel's ability placed him in good position when a crisis occurred in the palace and because of his faith in God, a decree was made throughout the Kingdom that all should worship the God of Daniel.

Trust in God and be bold. You can do it. Reach out for those goals in confidence.

> Speak to people who already work in your chosen career. You may find they'll be more than happy to share their insight with you and give advice on entering the industry.

Competency Based Interview Tips

For questions such as: "Tell me about a time you faced a challenge in your workplace and how did you overcome it?" Answer like this using the STAR framework:

Situation

Describe the situation, giving context for your answer. Describe what you set out to achieve.

Task

Describe the tasks that were needed to resolve the issues.

Action

Describe your specific role in the situation. Use lots of 'I's'!

Result

Describe the results.

The same technique can also be used to answer interview questions.

SHOULD I CONTINUE WITH MY CAREER OR STAY AT HOME WITH MY CHILDREN?

"…Yes establish the work of our hands."

Psalm 90:17

I almost didn't include this question because it is such a controversial topic. A passive aggressive war is going on between the mothers who supposedly don't love their children enough to stay at home with them and the mothers who apparently sit at home all day watching TV programmes and playing with glitter. I can't answer this with a prescriptive right or wrong answer but can only say you need to do what's best for you and your family.

Some mothers work because financially they can't afford not to whilst others don't work because the childcare costs would outweigh their salary. Again some mothers don't work because they want to be at home with their children whilst others work because they believe that the time spent away from their children helps them to be a better mother.

I work part time in an office and have a little business that I do from home (and I write!). I feel that this balance works best for me and my family. I have an income, I'm able to have adult conversations in the office and I learn new skills all the time. At the same time I have time to complete all my wonderful household chores, I can take the kids out to play in the middle of the afternoon if I want and I can dedicate as much or as little time as I want to my business and other projects in the pockets of time that can be carved out throughout the day.

For me, it has been important to remain in the workplace after children as in a recent job interview I was asked why I had worked in some of the roles I had, considering my qualifications and the role I was currently applying for. I responded that I simply took on jobs that allowed me to re-enter the workplace quickly after having children even if they were entry-level and it seems that the interviewer understood that. However, the significance was not lost to me that having a long career break can make it difficult to find work when one is ready to embark on a career again.

Prayerfully consider what's best for your family as you make this decision. Whether you choose to stay at home or go to work, know that each decision will require sacrifices. Don't be afraid to make that sacrifice, don't be afraid to take that bold step, it will work for you.

"And we know that God causes everything to work together for the good of those who love God and are called according to His purpose for them."

Romans 8:28 (NLT)

> Do what is best for you and your family. Don't worry about anyone else's opinion.

I WANT TO START MY OWN BUSINESS. HOW DO I GO ABOUT IT?

She makes linen garments and sells them and supplies the merchants with sashes.

Proverbs 31:24(NIV)

Firstly, what can you do? What skill or talent can you utilise? Can you write, draw, bake, dance, sing, design, babysit, teach, cook, clean, paint and decorate, DIY, entertain, drive, buy and sell, do makeup, hair, fitness, sew, model, photograph or plan?

Most businesses are an improvement on an existing idea or offer a niche on an existing product or service. You don't necessarily need an original idea.

There is a new category of business owners called 5-9'ers. These are people who work full time in 9-5 jobs then work on their own businesses at the evenings and weekends. You can start a business alongside your main source of income to minimise the risk financially and give the business time to grow.

I've heard it said that one in two businesses fail in their first year so why not start two! The Proverbs 31 woman had several business interests; selling merchandise, sewing linen garments, farming and wine making. Once you have established your business consider opening an additional business perhaps in a related area to the first business, this strategy will provide you with multiple income streams. Speak to existing business owners, undertake market research and write down a business plan. Many councils offer free courses to residents interested in starting a business, there are also many helpful resources online.

"And you shall remember the Lord your God, for it is He who gives you power to get wealth…"
Deuteronomy 8:18

Above all else, glorify God because it is He who supplies the power that is needed to make your business a success.

Starting a business is naturally risky. Don't feel fearful; know that God is in control.

Business Plan

1. **Business Summary** (write this last!)

2. **Products/services**
Describe your products or services

3. **Market**
Who are your customers? Where are they? Do they already buy the product/service? Have you got a customer base?

4. **Market Research**
-Desk research (Internet, current trends,quantitative data)
-Field research (Customer questionnaires/interviews, test trading)

5. **Marketing strategy**
Your method and cost i.e. social media which is free to a point, or print, t.v or radio advertising which have attached costs.

6. **Competitor Analysis**
-Name, location, size
-Product/service
-Price
-Strengths and weaknesses

7. **SWOT Analysis**

Strengths	Weaknesses
Opportunities	Threats

What is your USP? (Unique Selling Point)

8. **Operations and Logistics**
-Production
-Delivery to customers
-Payment methods and terms
-Suppliers
-Premises
-Equipment

-Management and staff

9. **Pricing**
-Product/service cost
-Cost per unit
-Price per unit
-Profit margin (£) and (%)

HOW CAN I EXCEL IN MY STUDIES?

"Intelligent people are always ready to learn. Their ears are open for knowledge"

Proverbs 18:15 (NLT)

For this question I decided to turn to my husband who has always done well throughout school and achieved a first class in his undergraduate degree. This is what he had to say on the matter:

"I was disciplined and I was focused and I had a purpose in life. Without purpose you can't achieve anything meaningful. So with good grades you can get a good job. I had a purpose to work in business intelligence as a business consultant and that's what I worked towards.

I attended all my lectures, I paid attention in lectures, and I completed all my homework and assignments.

I studied in the night, as that's naturally the best time for me to study. I exercised good time management as I had a lot of church commitments in the day and evening so I preferred to study at night. I also had good study skills. I know my greatest advantage is to listen to lectures, I don't take a lot of notes in class but I go over my notes straight after lectures. I like to explore so if I'm taught one topic I will go and research around the topic. I do extra work on my own.

I also didn't get too involved with hanging around with friends instead of attending lectures, this is all part of discipline.

However the most significant strength behind my grades was my service in church and deadly commitment to the things of God because I love God. "

So there you have it, one person's secret to good grades is a commitment to serving God and rigorous discipline. The Bible says "**Seek ye first the kingdom of God and all these things shall be added to you…**"(Matthew 6:33)

> Discipline is key to success in your studies.

Stephanie Ahemor

Additional resources
<u>Websites</u>

www.startups.co.uk

<u>Books</u>

Build a Business from your Kitchen Table

Sophie Cornish and Holly Tucker

Anyone Can Do It: Building Coffee Republic from our Kitchen Table

Sahar and Bobby Hashemi

Health and Lifestyle

HOW DO I INCORPORATE A HEALTHY DIET INTO MY LIFESTYLE?

"Or do you not know that your body is the temple of the Holy Spirit who is in you…"

1 Corinthians 6:19

Well, well, well. It's been less than a week since I completed a lengthy fast with my fellow church members. During that fast I was very proud of myself of being able to be disciplined towards food especially as it's been a while since I've able to participate fully in the fasting due to pregnancy and breastfeeding. I told myself after the fast that I would create some new good food habits and would not go back to being a serial snacker. Unfortunately, six days in and I've fallen off the bandwagon!

However, I've resolved to eat better. I know that I don't need to consume as much food as I do, my body can function just fine.

There are several approaches to having a healthy diet. You

can take the stance that you are going to be more mindful of what you eat and what you put into your body. Although having chocolate biscuits for breakfast on the train on the way to work (guilty!) may be quick and convenient think about the impact it will have on your body, your body deserves better. Why not wake earlier to have breakfast at home or prep something, i.e. yoghurt, granola and frozen berries which can be taken with you? Or even buy a box of cereal and keep it at work to have breakfast when you get into your workplace.

This approach requires you to be disciplined with yourself as you are the one holding yourself accountable.

Another approach is to become part of an online community. There are many that can be found online which can cater to your individual needs through the cuisine it provides recipes for or by the recipes being quick and easy to make. Another option is joining a well-known weight loss group such as Slimming World or Weightwatchers. It is the same concept of being accountable to a group during weight loss which maintains motivation and also being guided to make the right food choices. I have a friend who has had great success with Slimming World, attending regular meetings has helped her to lose a significant amount of weight and has kept her on track with her weight loss goals.

Also, recognise that it is not only over-eating that can be a problem but undereating too. Your body deserves better than to starve all day because you are too busy with work to remember to eat. Put yourself first. Take time out to mindfully sit down and eat, nourishing yourself in the process.

"Or do you not know that your body is the temple of the Holy Spirit who is in you, whom you have from God, and you are not your own? For you were bought at a price; therefore glorify God in your body and in your spirit, which are God's."

1 Corinthians 6:19,20

Your body is a vessel of the Holy Spirit, so accord it the due attention, care and respect it needs. Take care of yourself , you deserve it .

> Make yourself accountable to your
> weight loss. Start a group with friends,
> download an app to track your food or
> keep a food diary.

10 Portions of Fruit and Vegetables

Latest advice from scientists recommends that we eat 10 portions of fruit and vegetables a day in order to reduce the millions of premature deaths that occur each year.

Everything listed below provides one portion towards your needs for the day.

- 2 kiwi fruit
- 1 apple
- 1 pear
- ½ a grapefruit
- 8 cauliflower florets
- 1 glass of orange juice
- 3 tablespoons of peas
- 2 broccoli spears
- 1 tomato
- 1 banana

- ½ an avocado
- 1 sweet potato
- 2 tablespoons of cooked spinach
- 1 tablespoon of raisins
- 2 plums

HOW DO I INCORPORATE EXERCISE INTO MY LIFESTYLE?

"She sets about her work vigorously; her arms are strong for her tasks."

Proverbs 31:17 (NIV)

Try a little and often approach. You may not have time to go to the gym in the morning before work or be able to attend a cardio class in the evening but you can squeeze in little nuggets of exercise throughout the day.

In the morning try doing some stretching exercises as you get out of bed to help you feel more energised. Run up and down on the spot or do some squats as you're waiting for the kettle to boil.

Use the stairs instead of the lift when out and about. Put a YouTube video on and exercise in front of the TV or laptop when you get a minute in the evening. Go for a family walk or bike ride at the weekend. Go for a prayer walk at dawn.

Make it fun and you'll soon start to see a difference as you get fitter and fitter.

> Exercise in small bursts whenever you get the opportunity.

IS IT VAIN FOR ME TO CARE ABOUT MY OUTWARD APPEARANCE?

"Charm is deceitful and beauty is passing…"

Proverbs 31:30

No, I don't think it's vain to care about your outward appearance. It's good to take care of yourself and it often works out that when you look good, you feel good too.

It's nice to look nice, right? Just be careful that it doesn't become your main preoccupation. Beauty will pass so don't invest your all into how gorgeous you look once your make up is applied just right and you've got your new Peruvian wig on. It's not sensible to put all your confidence into your outward self. Instead look at the beauty of your inner spirit. It is your inner self, your conduct and behaviour that can compel and convict someone to act for you, not your outward self.

"Do not let your adornment be merely outward — arranging the hair, wearing gold, or putting on fine apparel — rather let it be the hidden person of the heart, with the incorruptible beauty of a gentle and quiet spirit, which is very precious in the sight of God."

1 Peter 3:3,4

Appearance is so temporary, so don't make major decisions based on outward appearance. People age, lose hair and gain weight. So it is not the basis to make any final decisions on, such as marrying someone because of their six-pack, even that will fade away.

Commit to being more God-like and look at people the same way God looks at us, at the heart.

"Out of the abundance of the heart his mouth speaks" (*Luke 6:45*). It is from the heart that we know the true characteristics of a person. Remember this, as no matter how much time you spend investing in your outward self, your inner being, the true you will always shine out. You are going from glory to glory.

> Beautify your inner self. You are a pleasing aroma to God. *(2 Corinthians 2:15)*

HOW DO I NURTURE MY INNER BEAUTY?

"Rather let it be the hidden person of the heart, with the incorruptible beauty of a gentle and quiet spirit, which is very precious in the sight of God"

1 Peter 3:4

All of us have had varied upbringings, some with good experiences and some with negative experiences. Everything that we have gone through, the people we have encountered and the pain we've suffered has added up to make each person the unique individual that they are today.

Rather than feeling angry at a past incident we have to forgive and acknowledge that it has contributed to the making of who we are today. The Bible says that:

"All things work together for good for those who love God..."

Romans 8:28

Although circumstances may not have been ideal, everything comes together and works into God's plan.

Take some time to reflect on yourself, to analyse yourself and to question why you do the things you do and see if there is anything that needs to be improved on as well as recognizing your special talents.

Before I got married I decided that I would try to work on what I considered to be my major flaws, the main one of which was stubbornness! Although my aim was not to become perfect before marriage, as no human being can be perfect, by recognising that this was a problem for me, it meant that I was able to address it and any conflict that may arise from it during the course of day to day life.

You may have low self-esteem, you may be very fearful, you may have trust issues but you can overcome any thing that presents itself as a stumbling block in your life. You are a very special person and as a woman you are uniquely placed to have great influence over your entire household and your children, thereby influencing the next generation.

The Bible says that wives are able to win their husbands without a word but purely through their conduct (*1 Peter 3:1*). The influence that women yield is unique.

In nurturing your inner self, fill your heart and mouth with wisdom (*Proverbs 8:6*), be diligent and hard-working (*Proverbs 6:10,11*), be able to take instruction (*Proverbs 5:23*) and be God-fearing (*Proverbs 9:10*).

Above all, be yourself. God has created you for His glory. As you continue to grow both physically and spiritually, God will continue to perfect everything that concerns you.

> Let the love of God flow through you and make you glow.

I FEEL SO DOWN AND DEPRESSED. HOW DO I CLIMB OUT OF THIS?

My tears have been my food day and night while they continually say to me, 'Where is your God?'"

Psalm 42:3

At one point or another in life, the vast majority of people have suffered from a bout of depression. When are you feeling down and are struggling to make sense of life, yourself, the point of everything; then look for a word in scripture and stand on it. Know that this is God's word for you and that it is as applicable to you today as it was back then because the word of our Lord endures forever. (*Isaiah 40:8*).

David, of Biblical fame, was greatly distressed because the people spoke of killing him. However, he strengthened and encouraged himself in the Lord (*1 Samuel 30:6*). David trusted in God when his life was on the line and he did not give up hope. After strengthening himself in God, David was able to pursue the enemy and recover all that he had lost, not one single thing was lost.

We are loved by God and the Bible says that perfect love casts out fear. Meditate on the love that God has for you, it is all encompassing and it is perfect. Reject fear, reject torment and reject sadness. God has a great plan for your life that will surely come to pass.

"There is no fear in love; but perfect love casts out fear, because fear involves torment..."

1 John 4:18

Do not worry about tomorrow (*Matthew 6:34*) but take each day as it comes. Allow the awesome love of God to bring you out of darkness and into His glorious light.

> Reflect on what you DO have, not what you don't have.

HOW DO I OVERCOME LAZINESS/LACK OF MOTIVATION?

"Lazy workers are soon poor, hard workers get rich"

Proverbs 10:4 (NLT)

Do it, do it! Whatever your plans, hopes and dreams are; make it happen!

When it seems like it is too hard to achieve a seemingly unattainable goal it is easy to just give up or not even try and make the effort. But it is possible because **'everything is possible to him who believes'** (*Mark 9:23*).

Draw up plans for the ideas you have floating around in your mind. Work out which one is the most viable and practical to start with and work it through to completion. Carve out pockets of time to work in, whether it be on your lunch break at work or in the quiet of night.

Make the vision plain, write it down and run with it! (*Habakkuk 2:2*).

Stop talking and start doing! Don't be a defeatist but believe that the end goal is possible and start working towards it.

"Go to the ant, you sluggard!
Consider her ways and be wise,
Which, having no captain,
Overseer or ruler,
Provides her supplies in the summer,
And gathers her food in the harvest."

Proverbs 6:6-8

The ant is able to motivate herself to get her work done. She doesn't need a supervisor pushing her and telling her what to do because she knows that ultimately, her hard work will benefit her.

With man, what you dream of may not be possible but with God all things are possible. With the help of God you can achieve it. Believe in yourself and push, you can make it.

Make a plan, stick with it, and

don't give up!

I'M BURNT OUT. THERE AREN'T ENOUGH HOURS IN THE DAY. I'M STRUGGLING TO BALANCE MY SPOUSE, CHILDREN, PARENTS, WORK, BUSINESS, STUDIES, DOMESTIC RESPONSIBILITIES, MINISTRY, FRIENDS. I NEED HELP!

"...My grace is sufficient for you..."

2 Corinthians 12:9

I can only speak from my own experience but as a wife and mother there is a lot to do. This includes, but is not limited to, looking after my family, work, business, ministry, cooking, cleaning, laundry, grocery shopping, homework, volunteering, staying in touch with my extended family, catching up with friends, the list is endless...

In the past whenever I heard the word grace, I always thought of it as a lofty, intellectual concept. The meaning of grace is unmerited or undeserved favour. Grace was always an abstract concept to me. I knew its definition but it had no practical meaning for me in my life.

However, several years ago I had a revelation from God. During this period of my life our church was embarking on a season of prayer meetings every night for three months. At this time I also had a ten month old baby, was on maternity leave from a temporary job, my maternity pay had finished and I was trying to find a new job to return to work.

During the service I was meditating in the spirit God said to me ; 'Have you seen how easy it has been for you to get everything done over the last few days?' And I literally saw myself, in my mind's eye, over the last few days at home cooking, cleaning, taking care of the baby, working on whatever project I was working on (I always have one on the go); I saw myself being able to do all of the above without sweat and without complaint.

I understood that grace, practically and in reality, was being able to operate in one's calling almost effortlessly. Now of course everyone must put work into something they wish to get results from. There are no results without effort.

"But Jesus said to him, "No one, having put his hand to

the plow, and looking back, is fit for the kingdom of God."

Luke 9:62

You have to put the work in; but once you know what you are called to do with your life, with grace added to that knowledge, you are unstoppable. Nothing can hold you back.

I think the feeling of being burnt out comes from a frustration of not knowing what your calling is. Due to this, your energy can be used up in so many places, you find yourself being spread too thin and you begin to despair because you feel like a hamster churning away all your energy but never making any advancement.

After this revelation, I began to feel more settled knowing that wherever God placed me and whatever He asked me to do, He would also equip me for the assignment by giving me divine grace.

If you ever feel like everything is coming down on top of you just know that the grace of God is sufficient for you.

"...And God is faithful; he will not let you be tempted beyond what you can bear..."

1 Corinthians 10:13

> Don't stress, trust in His grace.

Spiritual

Growth

HOW DO I PRIORITISE QUIET TIME FOR PRAYER AND PERSONAL BIBLE STUDY?

"Then you will call upon Me and go and pray to Me, and I will listen to you. And you will seek Me and find Me, when you search for Me with all your heart."

Jeremiah 29:12,13

Prioritise time with God by recognising the importance of it. You feed from the word of God and it is important to keep your spirit-man built up.

There are so many different competing priorities in life that it is easy to let your spiritual life fall by the wayside. After all it is the one thing that won't make demands of you if you neglect it.

Create a regular and consistent time to pray and read your Bible. Find the best time for you. For some it may be in the early in the morning before getting up for work, for others it may be in the night when the rest of the household is asleep.

Luke chapter 10 narrates Jesus entering the home of two sisters Mary and Martha. Mary sat at the Lord's feet and listened to what He was saying whilst Martha busied herself around the house serving. When Martha complained to Jesus that Mary was not helping her, Jesus responded;

"...Martha, Martha, you are worried and troubled about many things. But one thing is needed, and Mary has chosen that good part, which will not be taken away from her."

Luke 10:41, 42

Of course it is important to get all your chores done and to be hospitable to guests, but Jesus said what is actually most important is the word of God. The word of God is the 'good part' which Jesus referred to. The word of God is spirit and life *(John 6:63)* and it is also eternal life *(John 6:65)*.

Don't underestimate the importance of nourishing your spiritual life. If you find motivating yourself to pray alone difficult, try teaming up with a friend to pray over the phone, both of you taking it in turns to lead topics.

There is a time for quickly reading your Bible to gain words of inspiration for the day and a time for more in depth Bible study; where you sit down with pen and paper, a Concordance (or Google!) and take your time to expound the word of God. I pray that the Holy Spirit will give you new insight and a deeper revelation of the word as you study.

> Why not find a friend who can be your prayer partner? Set a regular time to pray such as a weeknight at 10pm over the phone.

HOW DO I SPEAK TO PEOPLE ABOUT CHRIST?

He said to them, 'Go into all the world and preach the

gospel to all creation'"

Mark 16:15 (NIV)

We are mandated as believers to share the gospel with everyone. The Bible says:

"**For, 'Everyone who calls on the name of the Lord will be saved.' How, then, can they call on the one they have not believed in? And how can they believe in the one of whom they have not heard? And how can they hear without someone preaching to them?"**

Romans 10:13,14

In order for others to receive the gift of salvation, the word of God must be spoken to them. If you are a Christian then it is more than likely that somebody spoke to you about Christ, someone invited you to church, somebody made a decision to share the good news with you which led to you having a relationship with God.

Having received the gift of salvation and all of the benefits that come with it, eternal life, peace, joy, the love of God, the blessings of God and being adopted by a heavenly Father, I can only surmise that it would be selfish of me not to share the means of accessing our Father in heaven through Jesus Christ with people that I meet. Not everyone is receptive when they hear the Word but I can guarantee that a seed is sown every time you speak to someone about your faith. What can present as hostility in a person can actually be doubt as they begin to question their own beliefs, years later they may find themselves in a church and open themselves up to the Holy Spirit finally understanding what you were witnessing to them about all those years ago.

So be bold, don't be afraid. Strike up a conversation anywhere, in the supermarket, at the office, at a family party or when meeting a new visitor after church. Don't think that you have to quote passages of scripture before you evangelise. Just a heartfelt re-telling of how you came to know Christ can be enough to start someone on the journey to building the most important relationship of their lives.

Share your testimony with someone, tell them how you came to believe, it's a great conversation starter.

Salvation Prayer

If you want to accept Jesus Christ into your life today and spend eternity with Him in heaven, then pray this prayer today:

"Lord Jesus;

I believe in my heart that you died and rose again to save me from my sins. I invite you to come into my heart from today. Lord, forgive me of my sins, I vow from today to make you the Saviour of my life. I will follow you for the rest of my days.

Thank you Jesus."

Amen.

HOW DO I UNCOVER MY PURPOSE/DESTINY IN LIFE?

"The Lord has made everything for its own purpose..."

Proverbs 16:4

Until you know your purpose in life one can often feel aimless, locked in a hamster wheel and unsure of where to get off.

John C. Maxwell describes in his book Work@Life how to uncover calling. There are two methods of determining one's path in life.

CERTAIN PATH

Sometimes God calls us by making things so obvious and certain that to not engage with the calling would be near impossible.

We may have a God given ability that we are born with such as music or design or a long held family business may be waiting for you to take over as successor.

ARRANGED PATH

The calling of an arranged path does not give room for choice or ambiguity. It is often clear to those around you that it is the path which you are meant to take.

The options with this path are limited. The choice is not about *what* to do but *whether* to do it. It is about determining how one should act upon realisation.

However you find out your purpose, whether it be continuing with the path you always seem to be drawn to or whether you explicitly know through a word from God, know this:

Don't leave the worst of yourself for God. Don't plan to serve God once you have given the best of yourself to your career, to your family or to making money. God deserves the best of you.

"Remember your Creator in the days of your youth, before the days of trouble come and the years approach when you will say,

"I find no pleasure in them""

Ecclesiastes 12:1 (NIV)

A time will come when you are old, feeble and tired. Is that the 'you' that you will use to serve God? What will your capacity be then? Your energy and usefulness will be limited. Your creativity and vibrancy will be long gone.

God's plan for you is time limited and then the opportunity will pass away. If you hear God calling you to do something, do it now! Don't worry about the how's, the why's and the where's. Just know that God will give you the grace that is needed to accomplish your God given task.

You don't know how many lives are reliant on your obedience. Be a destiny-changer, obey God now.

> Ask those around you what
> they think your talents are.

Additional Resources

<u>Books</u>
Life@Work: Marketplace success for people of faith, John C. Maxwell, Stephen R. Graves, Thomas G. Addington, 2005 publication

ABOUT THE AUTHOR

Stephanie Ahemor lives in London, UK with her husband and two children. She is a freelance writer who has written for various publications. She works in the communications and community investment fields. Stephanie has a degree in Law from the University of Kent.

www.ingramcontent.com/pod-product-compliance
Lightning Source LLC
Chambersburg PA
CBHW060019050426
42448CB00012B/2812